INSTANT CHRISTMAS PAGEANT:

The Mouse's Tale

by

Bob Latchaw

and

Cindy Hansen

Group

Loveland, Colorado

Group resources actually work!

This Group resource incorporates our R.E.A.L. approach to ministry. It reinforces a growing friendship with Jesus, encourages long-term learning, and results in life transformation, because it's

Relational
Learner-to-learner interaction enhances learning and builds Christian friendships.

Experiential
What learners experience through discussion and action sticks with them up to 9 times longer than what they simply hear or read.

Applicable
The aim of Christian education is to equip learners to be both hearers and doers of God's Word.

Learner-based
Learners understand and retain more when the learning process takes into consideration how they learn best.

Instant Christmas Pageant:
The Mouse's Tale

Credits
Edited by Christine Yount
Designed by Liz Howe and Diane Whisner
Cover illustration by Liz Howe
Interior illustrations by Leslie Clark

ISBN 978-0-7644-2352-9
15 14 13   13 12 11
Printed in the United States of America.

THE MOUSE'S TALE
Contents

HOW TO USE THIS
Pageant

Congratulations! Most of the hard work in preparing your children's Christmas pageant is already done! You hold the result of that work in your hands right now—*The Mouse's Tale*, an *Instant Christmas Pageant.*

The Mouse's Tale provides you with a complete Christmas program on compact disc. All the spoken dialogue, sound effects, and music are prerecorded. You even get songs for the whole congregation to sing along with the children.

This *Instant Christmas Pageant* is flexible. Your kids can perform it for

- a Sunday morning service,
- an afternoon or evening children's program,
- a family night program,
- a special Sunday school program,
- a nursing home program, and more!

And it can be performed by children from age four through eighty-four.

Even teenagers and senior citizens will enjoy putting on this pageant! Or you can have a puppet group perform the pageant.

The Mouse's Tale is easy to prepare. Just follow these simple steps:

1. Read the rest of this book, and listen to CD.

2. Photocopy the clip art on page 25 to decorate fliers, bulletins, and posters publicizing the pageant. Or use the computer clip art on the CD. Graphics may be used on any Macintosh with OS 8 or better, or PC-compatible running Windows 95 or better. Both platforms require a multisession-compatible CD-ROM drive.

3. Determine how you'll adjust the number of roles in the play to match the number of children who'll be in your program. On page 7 you'll find a few ideas on how to add to or subtract from the roles.

4. Have kids help you collect and create costumes and props. Many props may be collected from kids' homes. And the others may be created using the photocopiable patterns beginning on page 13. (These patterns are also contained on the CD. See step 2, above.)

5. Play the CD for your children. Then assign parts to children.

6. Practice the play with your children. Here's the fun part—kids don't have to memorize their lines! Don't have them lip-sync the parts, either. Instead, direct kids to follow the action and movement instructions in the script. After one or two times through, kids will know how to pantomime all the necessary actions. Or have kids come up with their own actions.

7. Perform the play. During the play, invite the congregation's participation in singing along with the Christmas carols.

It's that simple!

Here are a few tips to help you get the most of *The Mouse's Tale:*

1 ● Refer to the CD icon (see margin) to find exactly where a CD selection occurs in the pageant. Kids may easily practice their actions for a particular segment of the script with the corresponding CD track.

● Practice the actions and movements a few times so kids feel comfortable with their roles before a performance.

● Because each sanctuary setup is different, you may want to pause the CD during the pageant, allowing time for kids to move across the stage.

● Have a child or adult volunteer introduce the pageant before pressing the "play" button on your CD player. This is a good time to let the congregation know they'll be singing along during the pageant.

● Use teenagers, adults, or senior citizens to supplement roles if you don't have enough children.

● Increase the length of your program by having children read aloud sections of Luke's account of Jesus' birth before, during, or after the play.

● Read and discuss Luke 2:1-20 with your children as you prepare for the program. Use the costume-creation and rehearsal times as mini–Bible studies.

ASSIGNING THE
Roles

One of the best features of *The Mouse's Tale* is that almost any role may be played by any child in your church. Since the spoken parts are prerecorded and kids don't need to memorize lines, young children may play the main characters as easily as older children. The role of Granny Mouse is probably best suited to older children, however, since the suggested actions and facial expressions are more involved.

Each role in *The Mouse's Tale* is listed in the Creating Costumes section.

If you have fewer than twenty-two children, have only one camel, sheep, and shepherd. Or have the same children who play the sheep leave after saying their parts, change costumes, and return as camels. Or teenagers and adults may help by playing such roles as the three wise men, the shepherds, or Mary and Joseph.

If you have more than twenty-two children, increase the number of camels, sheep, and shepherds. Or form a separate children's choir to lead the congregation in singing the hymns.

CREATING THE
Costumes

Costume elements and props for each character are suggested in this section. Using the photocopiable patterns beginning on page 13, you may create costume elements such as mouse ears and sheep tails. (These patterns are also found on the CD.)

OLD GRANNY MOUSE—*Elderly member of the Mouse house. Down-to-earth, grandma-type.*

Suggested costume accessories: A shawl, glasses, mouse ears, and a tail. (See pages 13 and 14 for ears and tail patterns.) Has knitting needles, yarn, and a small suitcase. Dust hair with baby powder for a "graying" look. Use a black eyeliner pencil to make a black dot on nose and whiskers on cheeks.

YOUNG GRANNY MOUSE—*Granny Mouse as youngster. She appears during the flashbacks to the Christmas story.*

Suggested costume accessories: Wears a bow, mouse ears, and a tail. (See pages 13 and 14 for ears and tail patterns.)

JULIE MOUSE—*Granny's young granddaughter.*

Suggested costume accessories: Mouse ears, tail, mittens, and coat. (See pages 13 and 14 for ears and tail patterns.) Use a black eyeliner pencil to make a black dot on nose and whiskers on cheeks.

JOEY MOUSE—*Granny's young grandson.*

Suggested costume accessories: Mouse ears, tail, mittens, and coat. (See pages 13 and 14 for ears and tail patterns.) Use a black eyeliner pencil to make a black dot on nose and whiskers on cheeks.

STEVIE SPARROW—*Joey and Julie's young friend who doesn't believe in Christmas.*

Suggested costume accessories: A beak, mittens, and coat. (See page 15 for beak pattern.)

CLARICE COW—*The older keeper of the stable.*

Suggested costume accessories: All brown, all white, or all black. Wears a bell around neck, ears, and a swishy tail. (See pages 16, 17, and 18 for tail, bell, and ears patterns.)

DARRYL DONKEY—*He tells about giving Mary a ride.*

Suggested costume accessories: All brown, all white, or all black. Wears ears and a tail. (See pages 19 and 20 for ears and tail patterns.)

STAN SHEEP—*The more responsible member of the sheep trio.*

Suggested costume accessories: All white, along with ears and a tail. (See pages 21 and 22 for ears and tail patterns.) Glue cotton balls to ears.

SALLY SHEEP—*The second member of the sheep trio.*

Suggested costume accessories: All white, along with ears and a tail. (See pages 21 and 22 for ears and tail patterns.) Glue cotton balls to ears.

SAUL SHEEP—*The final member of the sheep trio.*

Suggested costume accessories: All white, along with ears and a tail. (See pages 21 and 22 for ears and tail patterns.) Glue cotton balls to ears.

SHEPHERDS—*People who come to see Jesus.*

Suggested costume accessories: A towel over head with a tie to secure it and a bathrobe. May carry a crook or old broom handle to look like a walking stick.

MARY AND JOSEPH—*Traditional Mary and Joseph remain at the stable during the entire pageant.*

Suggested costume accessories: A towel over head with a tie to secure it and a bathrobe.

ANGEL—*Guardian angel stands at the stable during the entire pageant.*

Suggested costume accessories: A white robe with gold tinsel. Attach gold tinsel to poster-board wings and a halo made out of a wire hanger.

CARL, CORY, AND CONLEY CAMEL—*The camels who bring the wise men.*

Suggested costume accessories: Brown clothes, huge sunglasses, ears, and a tail. (See pages 23 and 24 for ears and tail patterns.) For a hump, stuff towels or pillows in back of shirt.

THREE WISE MEN—*The three visitors who give gifts to Jesus.*

Suggested costume accessories: A towel over head with a tie to secure it and brightly colored robe. Each carries a gift.

PREPARING THE
Props

Most of the props you'll use in *The Mouse's Tale* may be created using the patterns on the following pages. In addition to these props, you'll need each character's suggested costume accessories, a rocking chair, a manger scene, a toy crib or cradle, and a doll to represent the baby Jesus.

Photocopy the following props on stiff paper and follow the instructions in the illustrations to create the props used in the pageant. The patterns are also available on the CD. Graphics may be used on any Macintosh with OS 8 or better, or PC-compatible running Windows 95 or better. Both platforms require a multisession-compatible CD-ROM drive.

MOUSE EARS

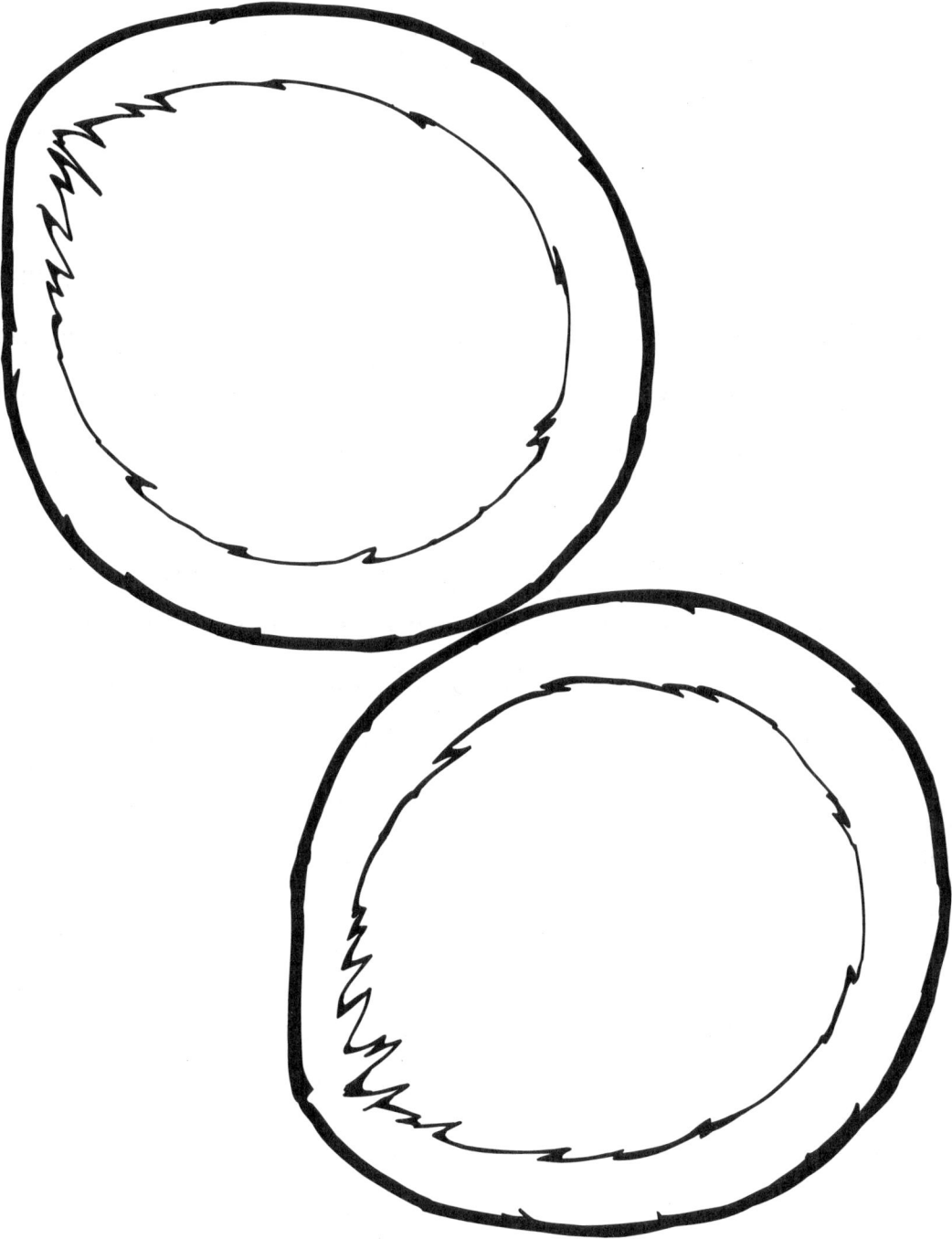

MOUSE TAIL

BEAK

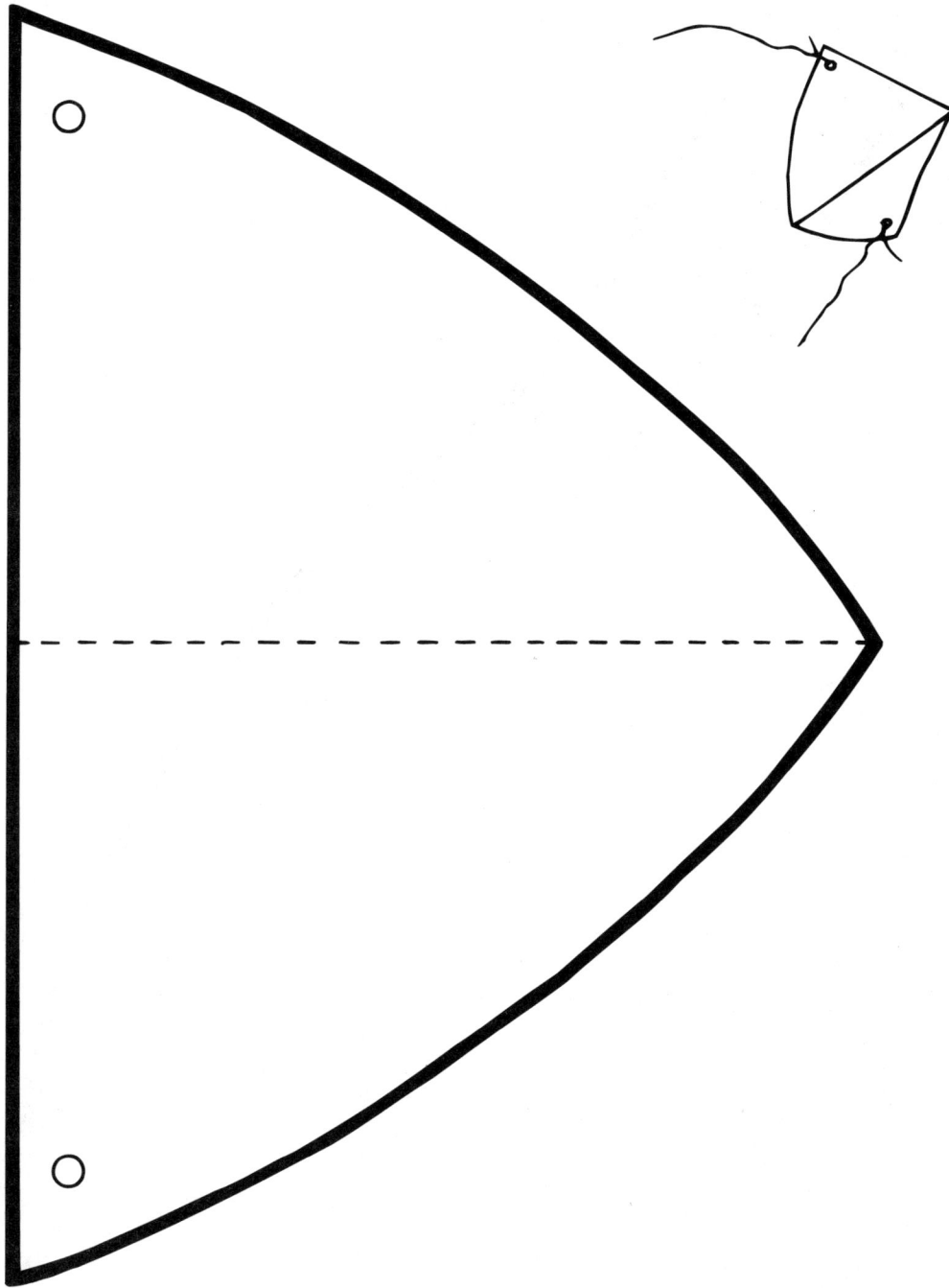

COW TAIL

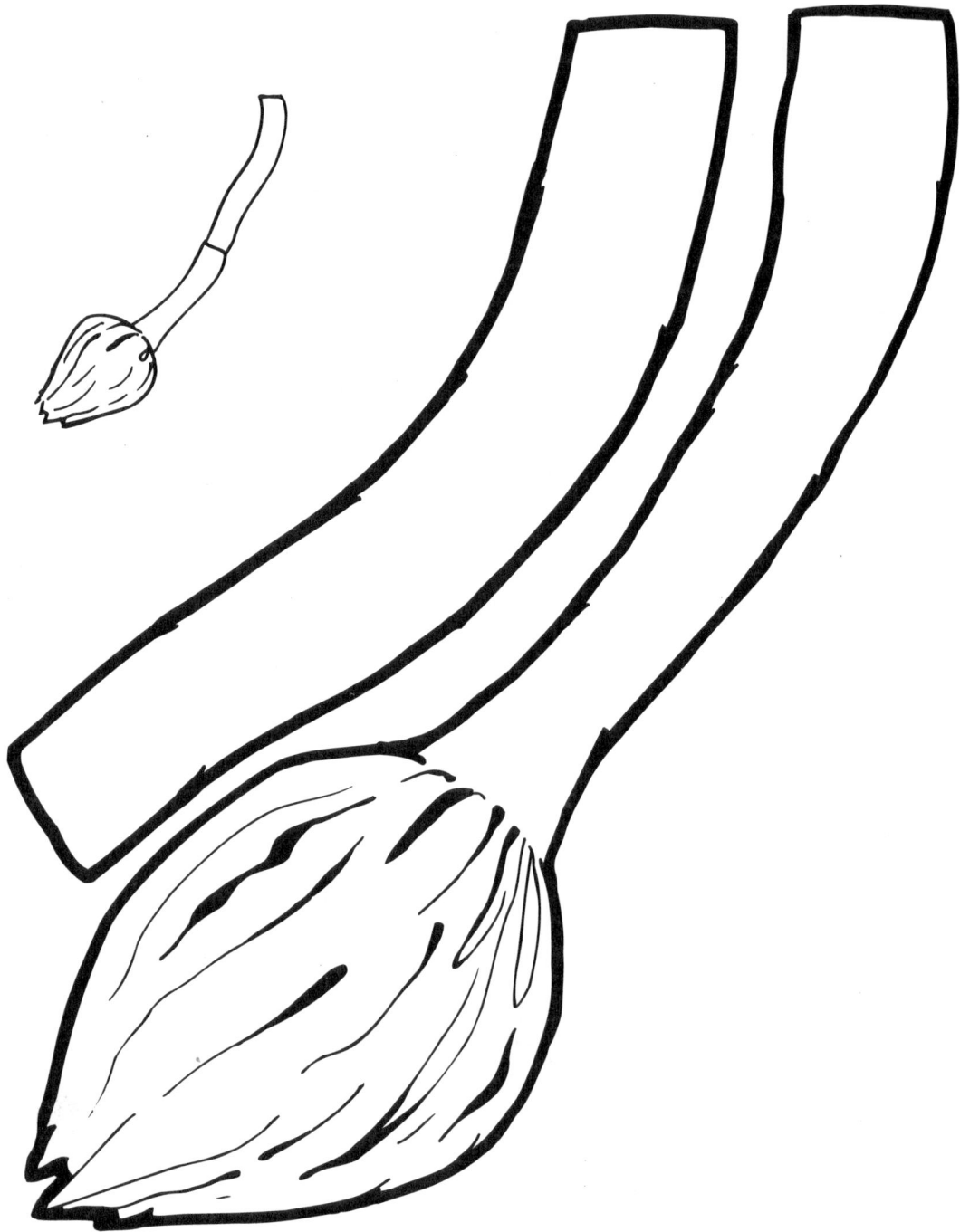

COWBELL

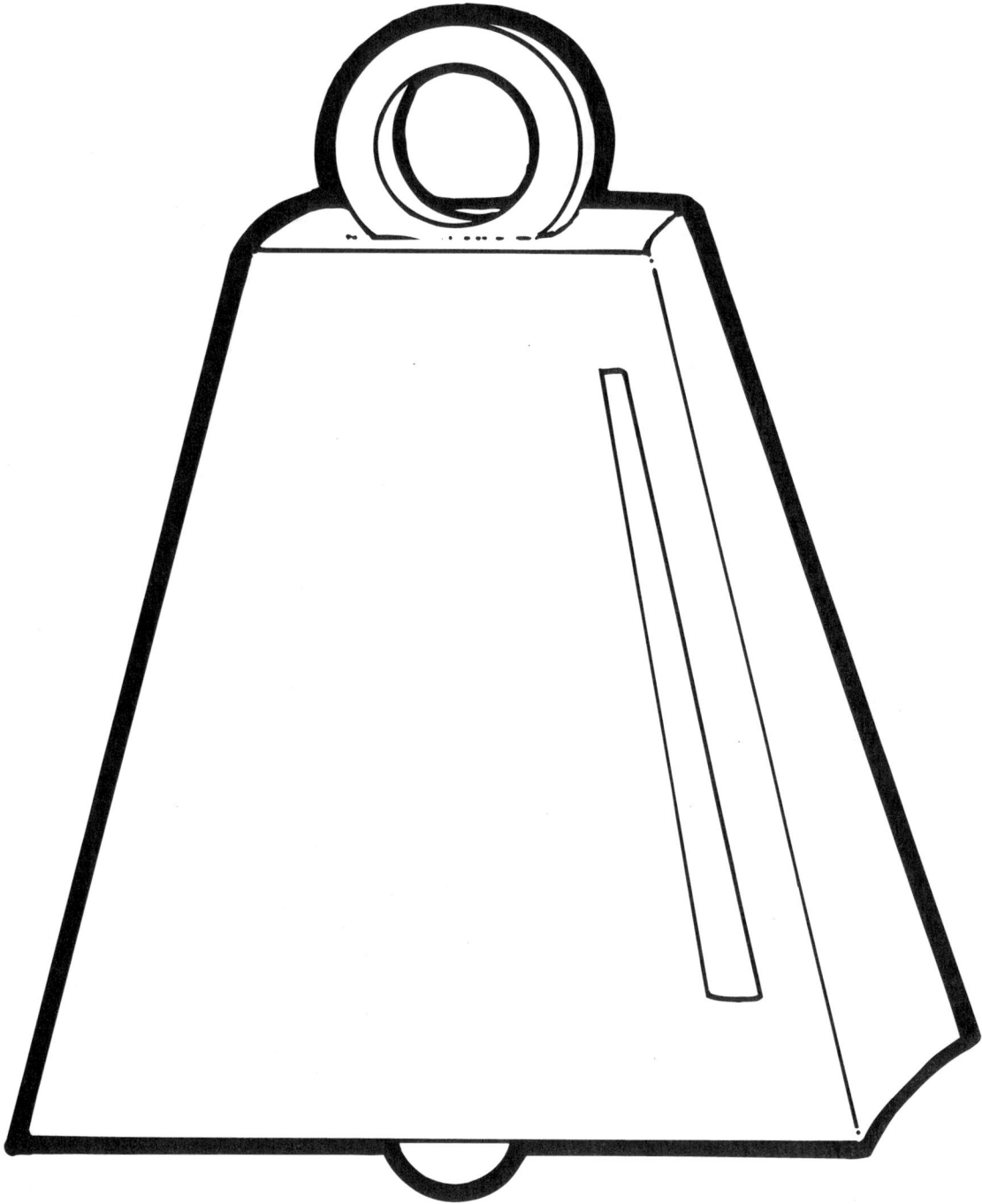

COW EARS

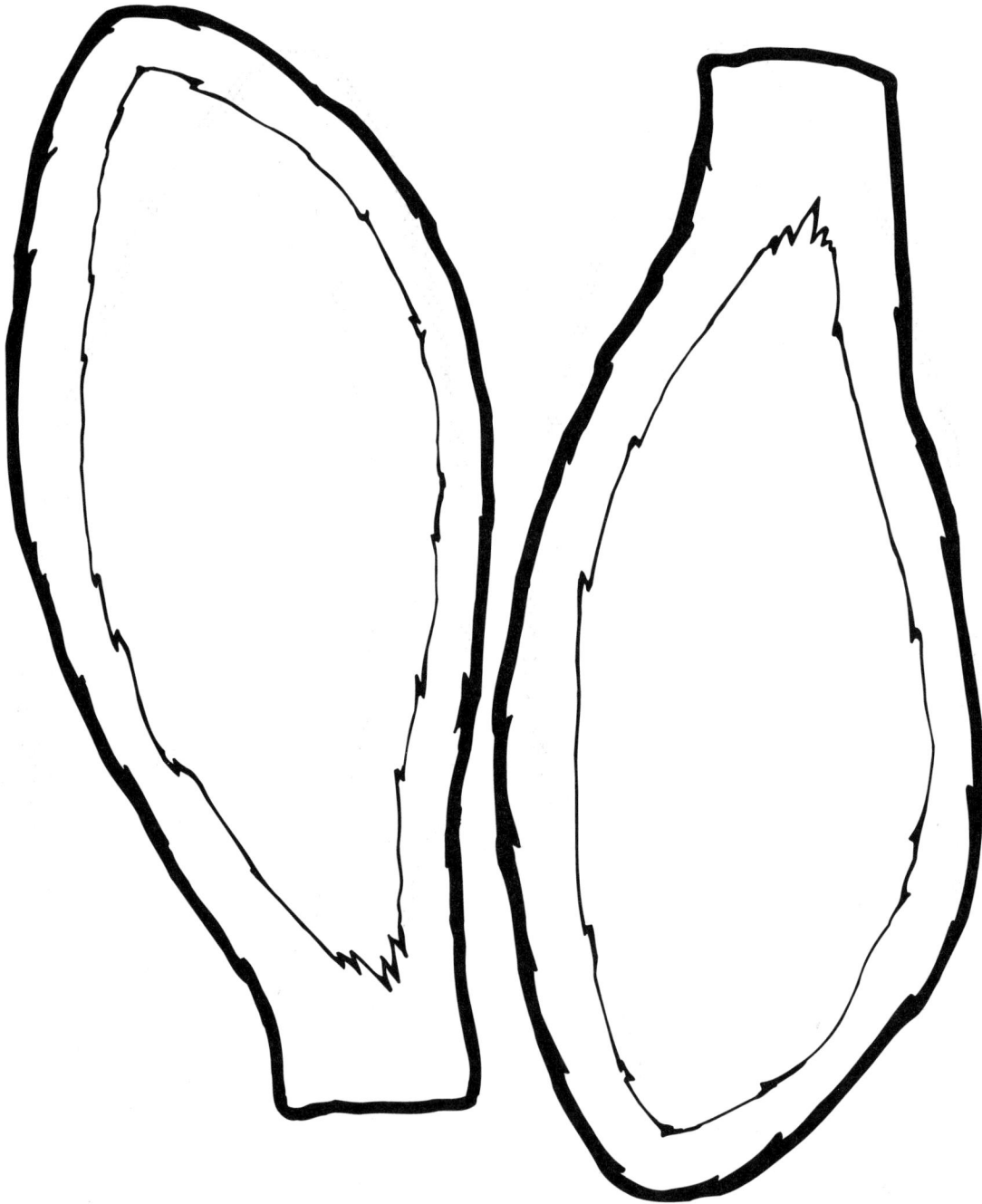

DONKEY EARS

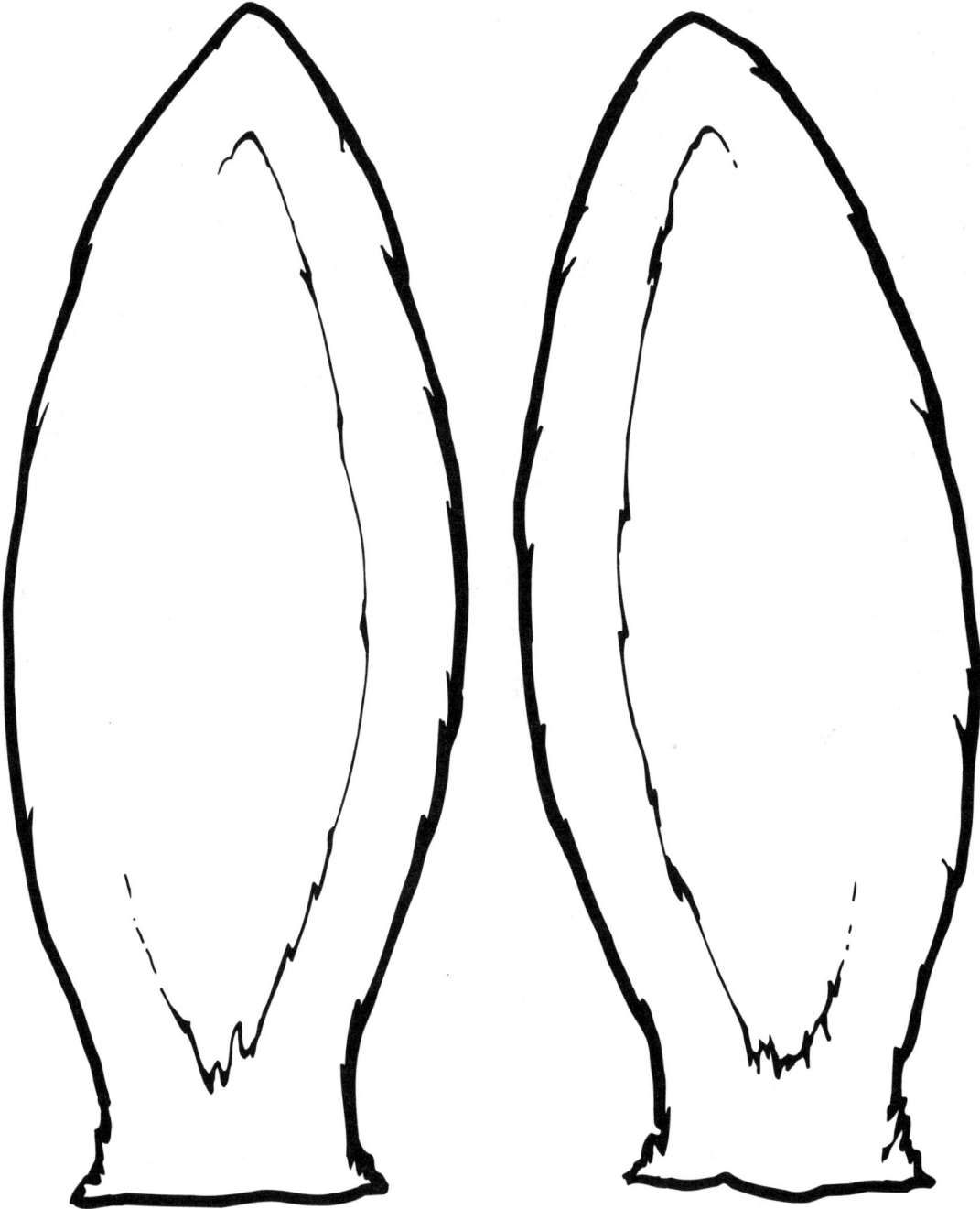

DONKEY TAIL

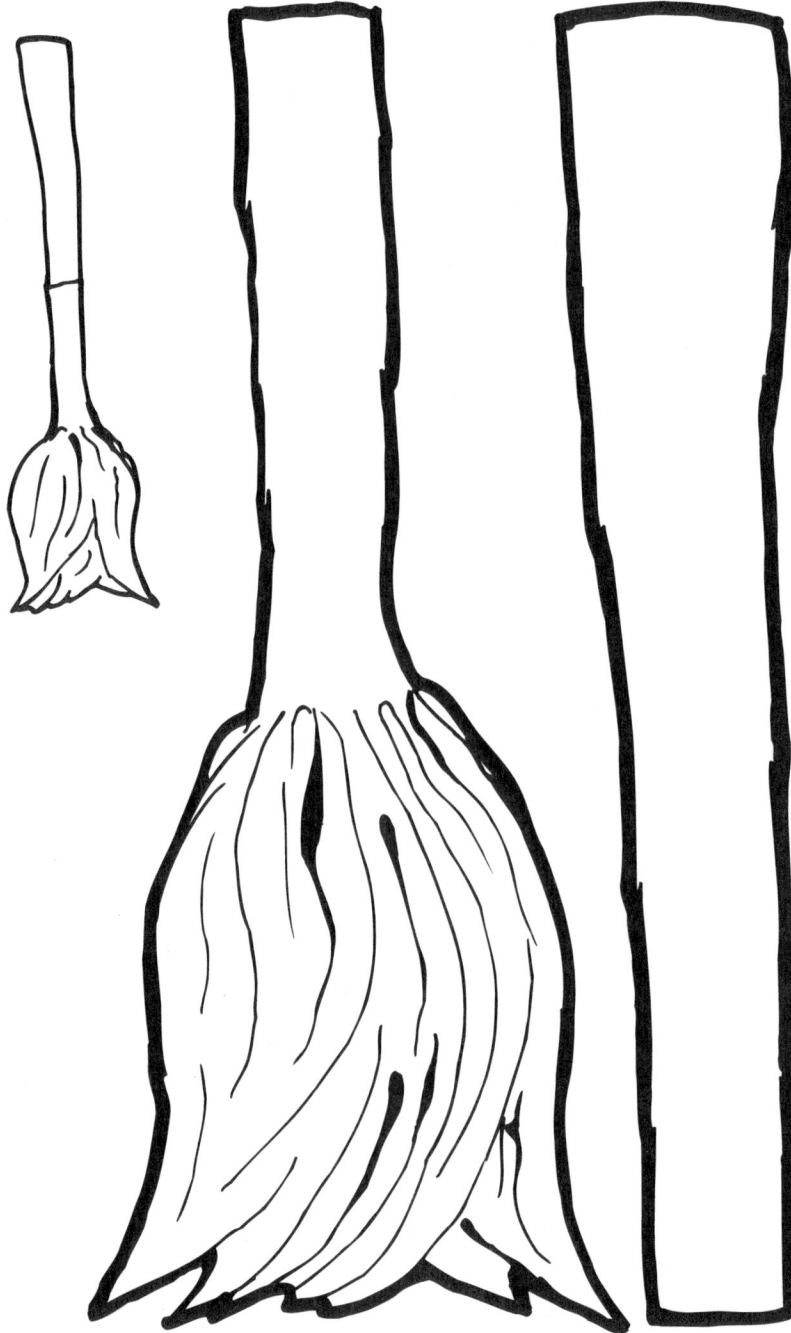

SHEEP EARS

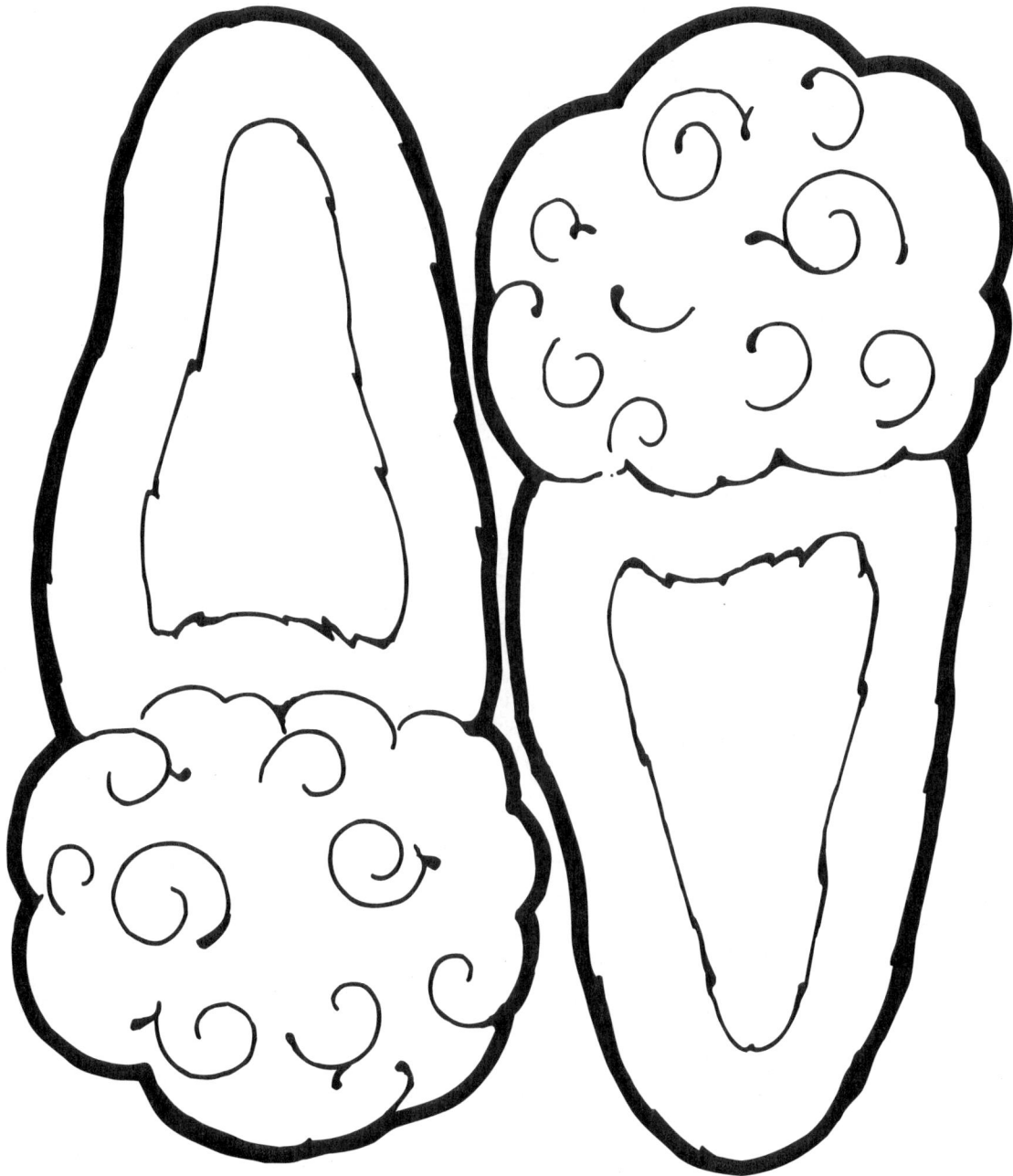

SHEEP TAIL

CAMEL EARS

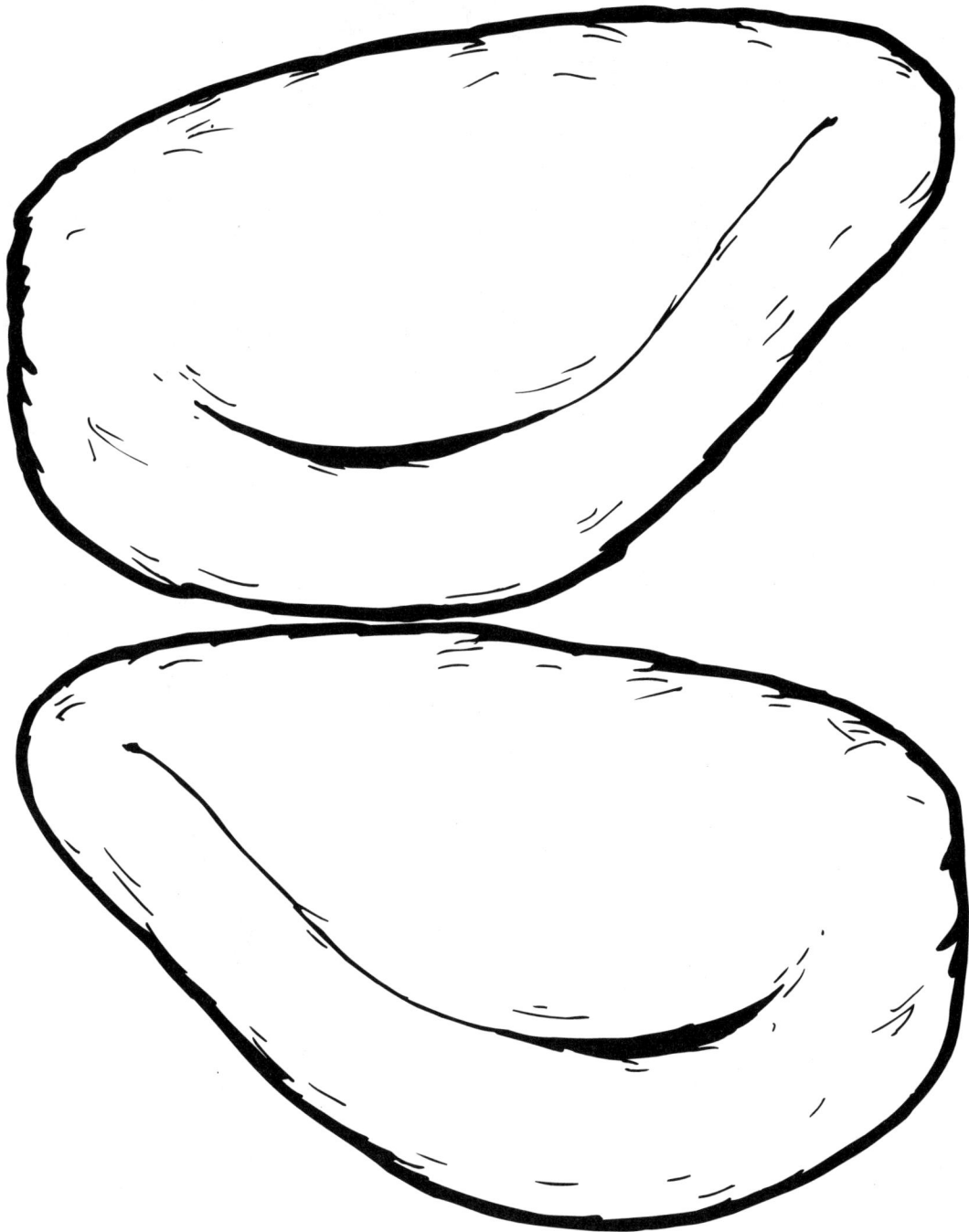

CAMEL TAIL

PUBLICIZING THE
Pageant

Photocopy the clip art on this page to publicize your children's performance of *The Mouse's Tale*. Use the clip art on fliers, bulletins, or posters. You also have access to the clip art through the CD. Graphics may be used on any Macintosh with OS 8 or better, or PC-compatible running Windows 95 or better. Both platforms require a multisession-compatible CD-ROM drive. Or simply add the appropriate performance information to the half-page flier below to use as a bulletin insert.

Date:

Time:

Place:

SINGING WITH THE
Congregation

The songs in *The Mouse's Tale* are familiar Christmas carols. But just in case some congregation members don't know all the words, photocopy the lyrics on page 48 and pass them out at the beginning of the pageant.

SETTING THE
Stage

Use the following diagram to set your stage. Adjust the location of the props according to the space you have in your church.

Place the rocking chair at stage left. Granny, Julie, Joey, and Stevie act in this area. The stable and manger are at stage right. Most action (animals conversing) takes place at center stage.

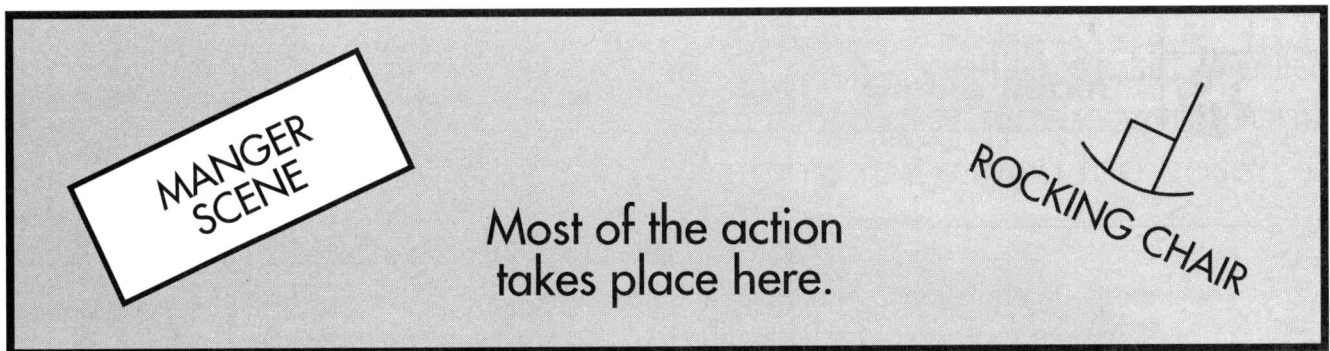

MANGER SCENE

Most of the action takes place here.

ROCKING CHAIR

AUDIENCE

THE MOUSE'S TALE
The Script

Use this script to familiarize yourself with the dialogue and actions in *The Mouse's Tale*. Remember, kids don't need to memorize these lines or even lip-sync the words with the CD.

Scattered throughout the script are suggestions to assist you in planning the movement and action for the Christmas pageant. Your kids may think up new ideas and actions—that's great! Incorporate their ideas into the pageant as much as possible.

Have someone introduce the pageant and remind the congregation that they'll be singing along with the carols during the program.

① OVERTURE *(Play as audience enters)*

②   ◆ **Old Granny Mouse enters stage left during the song.**

     ◆ **She sits in the rocking chair, knits, and hums the tune to "Hark! The Herald Angels Sing."**

     ◆ **Julie and Joey Mouse, Old Granny's grandkids, walk in from stage left looking dejected.**

OLD GRANNY MOUSE: ◆ **Looking up from her knitting.**
Well, hello, children! What are you up to? I figured you two would be out playing in the snow! Say now, why the long faces?

JULIE MOUSE: ◆ **Julie and Joey plop down on the floor beside Old Granny's rocking chair.**
Oh, Granny! We don't know what to do. We were playing with Stevie, the sparrow, and. . .

JOEY MOUSE: . . .and. . . and when we mentioned how much we were looking forward to Christmas. . .

JULIE: . . . and he said he doesn't believe in Christmas.

OLD GRANNY: ◆ **Stops rocking and lays her knitting in her lap**
Doesn't believe in Christmas? My lands, where did he get such a notion? You just bring your little friend in here, and I'll tell him a thing or two.

◆ Julie and Joey look at each other, smile, and nod.

JOEY: We knew you'd say that.

JULIE: Yeah, let's go get him!

◆ Julie and Joey leave stage left.
◆ Old Granny shakes her head, hums, and continues to knit.
◆ Julie and Joey re-enter stage left with Stevie.

OLD GRANNY: Hello, Stevie. Why don't you children sit down here, and I'll tell you about something that happened to me many years ago?
◆ Children sit beside Old Granny's rocking chair.
This was back when I was just a young 'un. Ever since then I've believed in Christmas—that God sent us his Son as a baby long ago.

STEVIE SPARROW: *(Unbelieving)* Yeah, right.

◆ Wind, night sounds, and flashback music begin. Old Granny speaks as she, Joey, Julie, and Stevie watch the action stage right.
◆ Young Granny enters stage right.

OLD GRANNY: It was a long time ago, and I was much younger then. I'd been traveling, and it was as cold as ice, so I ducked into a barn to warm up.
◆ Young Granny looks up, down, all around.

◆ Then she stoops and pretends to crawl through a hole.

◆ She bumps into Clarice Cow who is standing to the left of the manger, center stage.

◆ Mary and Joseph are standing by the manger, looking down at the baby. They don't notice the animal action in the stable.

CLARICE COW: Oh. What is? Oh, hello, Miss Mousie!

YOUNG GRANNY: ◆ Surprised and flustered

Goodness, I'm sorry. Please excuse me.

CLARICE: It's all right, Miss Mousie; don't worry about it. I'll tell you if I want you to mooooove.

◆ Embarrassed

Ooh, excuse me.

YOUNG GRANNY: Gee, thanks. I've been so cold, and I needed a place to get warm.

CLARICE: Well, you're not the only one. We've got other visitors in the stable tonight.

YOUNG GRANNY: Visitors?

◆ Granny looks around the stable.

CLARICE: Yes. You see, people from all over were in the marketplace today to be counted. The emperor wants to know how many people there are so they'll all have to pay him taxes.

JULIE: ◆ **From stage left, to Stevie**
That's the census we heard about in Sunday school.

STEVIE: Yeah. . . so what does that have to do with Christmas?

OLD GRANNY: I'm getting to that. Now you just be patient and keep listening, Stevie. Do any of you know the name of the town where this happened?

STEVIE: Yeah! Poughkeepsie.

OLD GRANNY: ◆ **Rolling her eyes**
No, not quite. Do either of you know?

JULIE: ◆ **Thinking really hard**
Ooh, ooh, ooh, ooh, I, got it, um uh. Jerusalem!

OLD GRANNY: No, but that's closer.
　　　◆ **Turns to audience**
How about any of you? Do you know the name of the town where the census happened?

◆ **Audience plant (if possible) calls out, "Bethlehem!"**

OLD GRANNY: Bethlehem? That's right. The little town of Bethlehem. Please sing with us.

❸ SONG: "O Little Town of Bethlehem"

❹ CLARICE: So you see, there are lots of people here because of the census. Every room in town is taken for the night.

◆ **Darryl Donkey enters stage right and stands by Young Granny.**

DARRYL DONKEY: You've got that right. We looked high and low for an inn to stay at, but we got the same answer everywhere.

CLARICE: "There's no room here! Moooooove on."
◆ **Embarrassed**
Oh, pardon me.

DARRYL DONKEY: Hee haw! Right! So the lady I was carrying and her husband. . . that's them over there. . .
◆ **Nods head toward Mary and Joseph**
didn't have anywhere to stay.

YOUNG GRANNY: So you ended up here!

DARRYL: Right! Hee! Haw!

◆ **Darryl sneezes.**

Excuse me!

YOUNG GRANNY: God bless you!

DARRYL: Thank you, must be the hay.

JULIE: ◆ **To Stevie**

Do you know where Christ was born?

STEVIE: In a hospital; where else?

OLD GRANNY: Actually, Stevie, he was born in a stable.

JOEY: In a manger.

JULIE: Yeah, away in a manger!

◆ **Turns to the audience.**

Come on, everyone, you know this one.

⑤ SONG: "Away in a Manger"

⑥ ◆ **When song finishes, Sheep enter one by one from stage right.**

◆ **Darryl watches and counts—getting sleepier all the time.**

◆ **Sheep move across the stage and stand with the other animals.**

DARRYL: Oh look, here come some sheep. One sheep. . .

◆ **Yawns**

two sheep. . .

◆ **Yawns**

three sheep. . .

z-z-z-z-z-z.

◆ **Snores until he is wakened.**

STAN SHEEP: Check it out. We're finally here!

SAUL SHEEP: Yeah!

SALLY SHEEP: Yeah!

DARRYL: ◆ **Waking up**

Uh? Wha? Shhhhhhhh! The baby is sleeping!

CLARICE: ◆ **Takes a step forward, with hands on her hips.**

Yes, hol. . . hold it down!

SAUL: Oops.

YOUNG GRANNY: Are you here for the census too?

STAN: Oh, no. Like, we're here to see the baby.

YOUNG GRANNY: How did you know about the baby?

STAN: Well, we were on a hillside outside of town earlier this evening eating. . .

SAUL: Eating!

SALLY: Eating!

STAN: It was a beautiful night, and the grass tasted great!

SAUL: ◆ **Saul rubs stomach.**
Great.

SALLY: ◆ **Sally rubs stomach.**
Great!

STAN: We were minding our own business, when there was a bright, wonderful light and a whole bunch of creatures up in the air.

STEVIE: ◆ **Covering his mouth as if scared, Stevie speaks from stage left to Joey and Julie.**
Angels?

JULIE: Yeah!

STAN: Our keepers fell to their knees in fear and wonder, and we heard about the birth of the infant king!

SAUL: Wow.

STEVIE: ◆ **From stage left Stevie scratches his head and speaks to himself.**
Hmm, I wonder what it would've been like to be there! I mean, to hear the angels talk.

OLD GRANNY: Oh, it would have been wonderful to hear them proclaim the birth of Christ the Lord.
◆ **Turns to audience**
Please, stand and join us in "Angels We Have Heard on High."

7 **SONG:** "Angels We Have Heard on High"

8 ◆ **Shepherds enter from stage right and stand next to Mary and Joseph.**

STEVIE: ◆ **From stage left**
Wow! Look, the shepherds!

JULIE: And angels!

STEVIE: Whoa!

JOEY: What a great welcome for the baby Jesus!

◆ **Funky music begins. Three Camels enter stage right followed by the three Wise Men carrying gifts.**

◆ **The Wise Men kneel by the manger as the camels join the animal crowd, center stage.**

◆ **Camels stand shoulder to shoulder as they tell their story.**

YOUNG GRANNY: Why, hello!

DARRYL: Howdy, strangers!

CLARICE: Oh, what's your story? Did you come to see Jesus?

CONLEY CAMEL: ◆ **Really cool**
Ready guys, let's kick it.

⑨ ◆ **Rap music starts.**

◆ **All three Camels gather to perform their rap. Camels stand side by side at the front of the stage and perform the following choreography for each verse:**

◆ **(After first verse, other characters join in the dance.)**

We been walkin' all day, and our hooves are beat.

◆ **Action: One step right, left foot step behind right foot, step right, put feet together, and clap at the same time.**

It's been a long time since we've gotten to eat.

38

◆ **Action: One step left, right foot step behind left foot, step left, put feet together, and clap at the same time.**

The guys on our backs say they got sore seats.

◆ **Action: Right foot out to right side, left foot out to left side— spread wide. Put hands on knees.**

Do the camel rap. Do the camel rap.

◆ **Action: Bend forward and shake the camel hump twice.**

◆ **Four measures of music without lyrics. Characters do their own actions.**

◆ **Do actions as described above during the singing.**

Our passengers came from a land afar,
Not just any men, three kings they are!
Instead of a road map, they follow a star.
Do the camel rap. Do the camel rap.

◆ **Four measures of music without lyrics. Characters do their own actions.**

◆ **Do actions as described above during the singing.**

We visited Herod on the way,
And this is what he had to say:
"Search for where the Christ child stays!"
Do the camel rap. Do the camel rap.

◆ **Four measures of music without lyrics. Characters do their own actions.**

◆ **Do actions as described on pages 38 and 39 during the singing.**

So here we are with our tale for you.

Three camels and kings and presents, too!

So listen in now, and hear the good news!

Do the camel rap. Do the camel rap.

◆ **Four measures of music without lyrics. Characters do their own actions.**

◆ **At the end everyone takes a bow and congratulates each other with handshakes, hugs, and high fives.**

10 **CLARICE:** Oh my, that was exhilarating. That really made me get up and moooove.

    ◆ **Embarrassed**

Um, excuse me.

DARRYL: Yeah, that was fun.

STAN: You guys really know how to groove.

SAUL: ◆ **Saul gives Camels thumbs-up signal.**

Yeah, groove.

SALLY: ◆ **Sally gives Camels thumbs-up signal.**

Yeah, groove.

◆ **The Wise Men present their gifts to Jesus.**

CLARICE: These three kings have come to worship the newborn baby and give him gifts.

    ◆ **Turns to audience**

Let's all stand up and sing this next song. Come on, get off your pews. Mooooove.

    ◆ **Embarrassed**

Ahem.

⑪ SONG: "We Three Kings"

⑫ CLARICE: Very nice, very nice. You may be seated.

OLD GRANNY: So you see, Stevie. The sheep and shepherds had heard the angels tell of Jesus' birth just as the prophets said it would happen.

JULIE: Then the shepherds and the wise men came to the stable, and they saw the child had already been born.

OLD GRANNY: And like most newborns, he would put up a bit of a fuss now and then.

    ◆ **Mary tries to comfort the baby.**

DARRYL: Gee, I wish we could help somehow.

CLARICE: Maybe if we sang, it would calm him and he would sleep.

◆ Clarice taps her finger on her chin as if thinking of a song.

Hmmm. I know.

◆ Opens her mouth and tilts her head back.

La, la, la. Yes, there it is.

◆ Music starts, and Clarice sings the first verse to "I Saw Three Ships." Clarice spreads her arms and sings like an opera singer.

◆ Music stops abruptly.

DARRYL: ◆ Shaking his head no.

No. that's not the right song.

He'd like this one.

◆ Music starts, and Darryl sings the first verse and chorus of "Go Tell It on the Mountain." Darryl taps his hooves to the music.

◆ Music stops abruptly.

STAN: That's cute, but I think there's a better one.

Check this out.

◆ Turns to the other sheep

Guys. . .

◆ Music starts, and the sheep sing the first verse and chorus of "The First Noel." Sheep snap their fingers in unison to the beat of the music.

YOUNG GRANNY: Well, that was good but. . .

◆ Music stops abruptly.

I think a quiet lullaby would be best.

◆ **Turns to audience.**

Let's all sing together.

13 **SONG:** "What Child Is This?"

14 **YOUNG GRANNY:** Look, he's asleep now.

◆ **Turns to audience**

That was a wonderful gift to give the baby Jesus.

◆ **Turns back to stable**

CONLEY: I wish I had a special present to give Jesus.

CLARICE: ◆ **Hangs head**

Me too.

STAN: A special gift? Yeah, me too.

SAUL: Yeah.

SALLY: Yeah.

YOUNG GRANNY: But all of you have already given Jesus wonderful gifts.

EVERYONE: ◆ **They all look at Young Granny.**

We have?

YOUNG GRANNY: Yes! You sheep gave Jesus the wool for his warm blanket. See how comfortable he is.

STAN SHEEP: ◆ **Looking proud**
You're right. And, and Clarice Cow, you gave Jesus your manger for his bed.

SAUL: Yeah.

SALLY: Yeah.

CLARICE: Yes, I did, didn't I?

DARRYL: What did I give to the baby Jesus?

YOUNG GRANNY: You carried his mother to Bethlehem. You gave her a safe and comfortable ride.

CLARICE: Yes!

CONLEY CAMEL: And the wise men couldn't have brought their gifts without us!

CLARICE: Yes.

DARRYL DONKEY: That's right. We all gave special gifts to the baby Jesus!

◆ **All animals proceed to the manger and look at the baby king.**

DARRYL: What a wonderful child! He looks so happy and peaceful there. Uh-oh.

　　◆ **Suddenly Darryl looks away from manger.**

Hee! Haw!

　　◆ **Darryl sneezes.**

Excuse me!

YOUNG GRANNY: God bless you!

DARRYL: Thank you, must be the hay.

　　◆ **Turns back to look at the baby**

Isn't he wonderful?

STAN: Yes, he is. You know, the angels we saw on the hillside said that the baby Jesus would bring joy to the world.

　　◆ **Turns to the audience**

Everyone knows this one. Come on; sing with us.

15 **SONG:** "Joy to the World"

16 　　◆ **As piano plays, Young Granny kneels by the manger and pretends to say something to the baby Jesus.**

　　◆ **The stable characters freeze in position.**

◆ The sound of a rocking chair, quietly rocking. Joey, Julie, and Stevie stand up and gather around Old Granny in her chair.

◆ She puts her arms around them.

OLD GRANNY: And so, children, that's what happened that night long ago.

JOEY: But, Granny, what gift did you give Jesus?

OLD GRANNY: Well, I promised him that if anyone ever didn't believe in Christmas, I'd tell them a little story—a story about a little baby who was born nearly two thousand years ago. I'd tell them about the most precious gift God ever gave us.

STEVIE: ◆ Scratching his head thoughtfully.
Jesus.

OLD GRANNY, JULIE, AND JOEY: Right!

OLD GRANNY: ◆ Turns toward audience
Now, every one of you join every one of us.

◆ All characters meet center stage and sing song together.

17 SONG: "O Come All Ye Faithful"

◆ At end of song, pause for applause.

⓲ EXIT MUSIC *(Plays as characters and audience exit)*

◆ Old Granny, Joey, Julie, and Stevie exit down center aisle.

◆ They're followed by the animals, wise men, shepherds, Young Granny, the angel, and Mary and Joseph with the "baby" Jesus.

THE END

O Little Town of Bethlehem

O little town of Bethlehem,
How still we see thee lie!
Above thy deep and dreamless sleep
The silent stars go by.
Yet in the dark streets shineth
The everlasting Light;
The hopes and fears of all the years
Are met in thee tonight.

O holy Child of Bethlehem,
Descend to us, we pray!
Cast out our sin, and enter in,
Be born in us today.
We hear the Christmas angels
The great glad tidings tell;
O come to us, abide with us,
Our Lord Emmanuel!

Away in a Manger

Away in a manger, no crib for a bed,
The little Lord Jesus laid down His
    sweet head.
The stars in the sky looked down where
    He lay,
The little Lord Jesus asleep on the hay.

The cattle are lowing; the poor Baby
    wakes,
But little Lord Jesus, no crying He makes.
I love Thee, Lord Jesus; look down from
    the sky,
And stay by my cradle till morning is nigh.

Angels We Have Heard on High

Angels we have heard on high,
Sweetly singing o'er the plains;
And the mountains in reply
Echoing their joyous strains.

Shepherds, why this jubilee?
Why your joyous strains prolong?
Say, what may the tidings be,
Which inspired your heav'nly song?

Glo————ria in excelsis Deo!
Glo————ria in excelsis Deo!

Glo————ria in excelsis Deo!
Glo————ria in excelsis Deo!

We Three Kings

We three kings of Orient are;
Bearing gifts we traverse afar
Field and fountain, moor and mountain
Following yonder star.

Glorious now behold Him arise,
King and God and sacrifice,
"Alleluia, Alleluia,"
Earth to the heav'ns replies.

O star of wonder, star of night,
Star with royal beauty bright,
Westward leading, still proceeding,
Guide us to thy perfect light.

O star of wonder, star of night,
Star with royal beauty bright,
Westward leading, still proceeding,
Guide us to thy perfect light.

What Child Is This?

What child is this, who, laid to rest,
On Mary's lap is sleeping?
Whom angels greet with anthems sweet,
While shepherds watch are keeping?
This, this is Christ the King,
Whom shepherds guard and angels sing:
Haste, haste to bring Him laud,
The Babe, the son of Mary.

So bring Him incense, gold, and myrrh,
Come peasant, king, to own Him:
The King of kings salvation brings,
Let loving hearts enthrone Him.
This, this is Christ the King,
Whom shepherds guard and angels
    sing:
Haste, haste to bring Him laud,
The Babe, the son of Mary.

Joy to the World

Joy to the world! The Lord is come;
Let earth receive her King;
Let ev'ry heart prepare Him room
And heav'n and nature sing,
And heav'n and nature sing,
And heav'n and heav'n and nature sing.

Joy to the world! The Savior reigns;
Let men their songs employ;
While fields and flood, rock, hills,
    and plains,

Repeat the sounding joy,
Repeat the sounding joy,
Repeat, repeat the sounding joy.

No more let sin and sorrow grow,
Nor thorns infest the ground;
He comes to make His blessing flow
Far as the curse is found,
Far as the curse is found,
Far as, far as the curse is found.

O Come All Ye Faithful

O come, all ye faithful, joyful and
    triumphant,
O come ye, O come ye to Bethlehem!
Come and behold Him, born the King
    of angels!
O come, let us adore Him,
O come, let us adore Him,
O come, let us adore Him, Christ
    the Lord!

Yea, Lord, we greet Thee,
Born this happy morning,
Jesus, to Thee be all glory giv'n;
Word of the Father,
    now in flesh appearing!
O come, let us adore Him,
O come, let us adore Him,
O come, let us adore Him, Christ
    the Lord!

Sing, choirs of angels, sing in exaltation,
O sing, all ye citizens of heav'n above!
Glory to God, all glory in the highest!
O come, let us adore Him,
O come, let us adore Him,
O come, let us adore Him, Christ the Lord!